THE REAL "LONG WAR":
THE ILLICIT DRUG TRADE
AND THE ROLE OF THE MILITARY

INTRODUCTION

As the Iraq and Afghanistan wars wind down, the U.S. military, like most other Western militaries, is enveloped in campaigns of reappraisal about what its role should be for the next few decades. The U.S. Navy and Air Force are developing the concepts of the Air-Sea Battle and Offshore Control, which are aimed essentially at countering the anti-access capabilities of nonstate, but especially state, adversaries. Since the unspoken focus of these concepts is on countries such as China or Iran, these are traditional military concerns and, to the extent that they facilitate the conduct of expeditionary operations, they will necessarily involve the U.S. Army, too. But there can be little doubt about the general Western distaste for another major, land-centric conflict for the next decade or 2; nor, given the characteristics of China and Iran, would this make much strategic sense. Accordingly, the issue of what the U.S. Army's priorities should be for the next decade arises.

Despite its probable institutional preference for a return to the land warfare-fighting ethos that preceded the current stress on counterterrorism operations, the Army is having to consider further engagement in irregular warfare and/or stability operations in its various guises. The so-called war on drugs will necessarily be a component of that much broader concept of future military operations, and from the U.S. Army's perspective, deserves reconsideration.[1] Yet, such a focus elicits opposition, first from those who

1

argue that the Army's greater engagement in the war on drugs would necessarily be an "exercise in futility"[2] and, second, from the argument that this mission is already catered for sufficiently. Any further investment in times of budgetary constraint, it is argued, would undermine the Army's core warfighting capabilities. The issue evidently demands serious thought.

This Paper will argue, first, that the scale of the threat posed to Western security by the illicit trade in drugs is sufficiently serious to warrant both the label of a "war" (if with some reservations and caveats) and the extensive involvement of the military. It will then explore the extent, and the limitations, of the military contribution to the war on drugs. The Paper will present some conclusions and a review of the implications of the war on drugs for the U.S. military of the 21st century.

SCALING THE THREAT

Introduction.

The misuse of drugs is not, of course, new. It has been endemic and regarded as a serious social problem in Southeast Asia and China, for example, for nearly 200 years. Nonetheless, the threat posed by the illicit trade in drugs is now on a scale never before experienced.[3]

The threat represented by the illicit drug trade is, moreover, a "wicked" one in that there are so many social, political, economic, and military dimensions to the problem that no quick and easy solutions seem likely to appear. It is thus a problem that needs to be thought about holistically. The Kenneth Waltz model of the three levels of security, that of the individual, the state, and the international system, is useful for helping do this.[4] (See Figure 1.)

	Demand	Supply (Production)	Supply (Transportation)
The Individual			
The State			
The System			

Figure 1. The Kenneth Waltz Model of the Three Levels of Security.

The result is a kind of matrix of aspects of the threat represented by the illicit trade in drugs to which the military can make a significant contribution (or not). In the nature of things, the military contribution will largely focus on the supply side of the business, rather than the critical matter of demand, but is important for all that. Such a matrix offers a convenient way of demonstrating the sheer variety of the military's contributions and of articulating the challenges it will face in doing so. The matrix also emphasizes the point that the military contribution is a necessary, but decidedly not a sufficient one; this in itself will pose the U.S. military a significant problem, an issue that will be discussed later.

Assessing the scale of the threat is complicated by the fact that the three levels of individual, state, and system are not discrete. In their nature and effect, they shade into one another; for all that, Waltz's three-fold approach remains a useful way of analyzing the issue.

The Threat to the Individual.

For the individual, the trade in illicit drugs may well be a matter of life and death. A particularly worrying development at this level of analysis is the rise in the manufacturing, trafficking, and consumption of methamphetamines, "ice," and other amphetamine type stimulants (ATS), especially in Southeast Asia, because the physiological impact of these is generally considered much more serious than that of heroin, cocaine, or cannabis.[5] More generally, there are two million drug addicts in Russia, and 30,000 of them die each year. As far as many Russians are concerned, therefore, security is not about the protection of Russian interests in Europe or other distant parts of the world, it is about what might happen to their family members in their street or apartment block, given the extent of drug use in their country. Much the same can be said for much of the rest of humanity.

The Threat to the State.

For the individual drug abusers, however, the need to finance their habit increases the level of crime, often producing vacuums of disorder within states where other forms of crime are likely to appear as well. In the 1980s, much of Colombia fell prey to this diffusion of social order. Over the past few years, significant areas of northern Mexico such as Chihuahua and Sinaloa have also degenerated almost into "no go areas" for government authorities.[6] This has resulted in over 45,000 deaths since 2006, mainly the result of feuds between different drug cartels or battles between them and the authorities.

Such no go areas can become mini-states within states, where the writ of the elected government does not run. In 1980s Colombia, the Revolutionary Armed Forces of Colombia (FARC) taxed drugs, producers, and traffickers, and became a quasi-administration that built schools and provided welfare programs. Likewise, Christopher "Dudus" Coke in Jamaica took over parts of the capital, stopped petty crime, and kept children off the streets after 8 p.m.[7] More prosaically, even the perception of lawlessness in one part of a country can damage the national economy by under-cutting investment, travel, and other legal business.[8]

Individuals pay taxes to the state in the expecta-tion that the state will look after them. When it fails to do so, its entire legitimacy is imperiled. A failure to deal with the drug threat, therefore, undercuts the social contract that binds the individual and the state together, and so destabilizes government. This pro-cess is especially rapid where the drug trade leads to the wholesale corruption of the politicians, adminis-trators, law enforcement agencies, and legal authori-ties of the state, for example, in South America and West Africa.[9] More insidiously, the penetration by illegitimate business into legitimate business contami-nates the second, while making the first harder to deal with. In Colombia, for example, the leaders of drug cartels took over much of the country's cattle ranching business for this reason and with this effect. In West Africa, successful drug traders often choose to invest their earnings into legitimate as well as illegitimate business, sometimes for purely commercial reasons.

There are clear linkages between the trade in illicit drugs and terrorism, both national and transnational. The close association between FARC in Colombia and the country's traffickers is well known.[10] This toxic combination resulted in between 100,000 and 200,000 deaths and the emigration and displacement of over five million people. [11] The "Shining Path" organization in Peru (and parts of Bolivia) is similarly financed, as is Afghanistan's Taliban, in its case from the opium business. Reports that al-Qaeda is increasingly seeking refuge in the ungoverned spaces of Latin America have accordingly alarmed many.[12] Al-Qaeda in the Maghreb [AQIM] appears to handle cocaine trafficking from West Africa and heroin from East Africa northwards across the Sahara, although it should be said that many suspect its ideological commitment; this may well be largely a legitimacy branding exercise by out-and-out criminals.

A problem in one country can easily spread in a variety of ways. One is when the trade within one country becomes associated with the citizens of another. The American pursuit of Jamaica's "Mr. Coke," for example, derived in large measure from the estimated 24,000 drug-related killings that Mr. Coke's alleged associates had been responsible for over the years within the United States itself. American foreign policy toward Central America has, for many years, been shaped by the perceived threat of the cocaine trade from that region. At the moment, the cost of the drug trade for the United States is estimated to be approximately 19,000 drug-induced deaths and $160 billion a year.[13] This and other consequences constitute "a serious threat to the national security of the United States requiring a concerted effort by all appropriate Departments and Agencies."[14]

International consequences can also result from the large-scale movement of people escaping from the collapsed and lawless area of one country into another neighboring country. The social challenges already faced by Ecuador have been greatly exacerbated by the arrival of 300,000 refugees from Colombia, for example. Again, Mexico's southern neighbors are vulnerable to Mexican drug trafficking organizations (DTOs) spreading their activities southward.[15] All of these undermine the stability of particular states as units in the system and thus may well constitute a threat to U.S. security, as well as to the system as a whole.

The Threat to the System.

Many of the DTOs are vertically integrated, which means they control all stages of the production and supply of drugs, and operate widespread transportation and financial support systems. The production and supply of illicit drugs is a transnational and truly global business that takes between 5 and 6 percent of overall world trade, slightly more than the value of the trade in cars and agricultural products combined.[16] According to the United Nations (UN), the DTOs generated $352 billion in 2008-09 and some $400 billion in 2010.[17] Drugs leaders such as Mexico's Ignacio Coronel Villareal have regularly been featured in the *Forbes* list of the world's richest and most powerful people.[18]

Because the drug trade is globalized, it becomes a systemic problem. In the 1980s, for example, the Colombian Medellin cartel imported semi-processed coca paste from Peru and Bolivia, processed it into powdered cocaine, and then transported it to the United States. This transnational activity was probably worth $4 billion per annum, more than Colombia's coffee and oil exports combined. The U.S. price of $18,000 a kilogram wholesale produced a fantastic return for investment, variously estimated at about

300 percent.[19] Similarly, Mr. Coke is held to be responsible for widespread mayhem in the United States and is believed to be connected to the United Kingdom's (UK) Yardie gangs. Such activities in fragile areas such as Central America, the Caribbean, and parts of Southeast Asia, Oceania, and West Africa undermine prospects for "a course towards stability and sustained economic growth that will build capital, attract foreign investment and overcome . . . current need(s) for external assistance."[20]

That West Africans and Iranians are now beginning to penetrate the Asia-Pacific Region and Oceania[21] demonstrates the increasing geographic spread of the drug trade; and as it spreads, it corrupts, like cancer. The sad current state of parts of Mexico reflects the fact that the country was once a transit area through which cocaine from Central and South America was supplied to the United States. Local criminals saw the benefits of participating in this traffic, especially when the cartels first paid for their services with cocaine rather than in cash. From the early 1990s, these Mexico-based organizations evolved into "vertically integrated multinational criminal groups," with distribution arms in over 200 U.S. cities.[22]

Much the same now appears to be happening in West Africa, an area, like northern Mexico, already under economic and social challenge.[23] A vicious circle may appear in which internal conflict and the rise of all forms of organized crime, the drug trade included, feed off themselves, especially when either is associated with the large-scale importation of firearms. Sometimes, indeed, the state may even come under the control of criminals as happened to Liberia under Charles Taylor (1997-2003) and very nearly to Sierra Leone under the Revolutionary United Front.

The destabilization of West Africa, an area from which the United States may need to draw up to 25 percent of its oil imports within the next decade, would have serious strategic consequences. This oil is "sweet" (with low amounts of sulphur), produced mainly from offshore rigs, which are safer than onshore equivalents and can be conveyed directly to the United States without choke points en route. There is evidence that South American cartels have moved into West Africa to expand their markets and improve access to Europe. There are also indications of specific links in West and North Africa between the drug trade and terrorists. Terrorists seem able to access the transport services offered by drug and other smugglers along the African coast and across the Mediterranean on their way to Europe.[24]

Were the drug trade to create conditions in which the security of this energy source becomes seriously imperiled, American (and other Western) interests would be seriously affected, hence the major investment in maritime security in the area in recent years. For the same reason, the European Union (EU) has become extensively involved in this area as well.[25] The drug trade creates systemic disorder most easily in fragile states, but when it affects increasingly important constituents of the system, such as Brazil and, indeed, Mexico, the systemic consequences become greater still.

Nor should the environmental consequences of the trade be forgotten. Two grams of cocaine consumed in Glasgow, Scotland, will have cost about eight square meters of Colombian rainforest. Over 20 years, Colombia has lost some 2.2 million hectares of rain forest to the production of cocaine and other illicit drugs. Environmentalists and human rights groups have concluded that settlers working for drug traffickers have been responsible for the destruction of nearly a fifth of the Maya biosphere rainforest in Guatemala since 1990, some 306,000 hectares being lost between 2001-06.[26] The "unrecorded tribes" of the area become victims, too.

In short, the effects and consequences of the drug trade are transnational and threaten the system itself, as well as individuals and particular countries, since the legitimate trade on which the system depends can only be conducted in conditions of reasonable social and political order, and it requires free and unimpeded access to the global commons. Transnational crime is a systemic threat because it threatens those commons. At sea, these threats include illegal fishing, people smuggling, arms smuggling in its various forms, piracy, terrorism, and the illicit drug trade. Although this Paper will concentrate on the latter, it is worth emphasizing the point that much of this may be interconnected. The rise of piracy off Somalia is due mainly to the breakdown in order in that unhappy country, to the illegal dumping of poisonous wastes in the country's waters, and to illegal fishing. The combination of these crimes have added up to the loss of some $300 million per year, which has ruined the Somali fishing community, thereby forcing the fishermen to seek other forms of livelihood. Unsurprisingly, the huge profits to be made from piracy have attracted many of these dispossessed fishermen, and their success has drawn in many others, further eroding good order within the state and damaging the international trade upon which the system depends. There are, moreover, often real links between the illicit trade in drugs and other threats against the system, most obviously its role as a source of finance for terrorism.

The interconnections between drug traffickers and other criminals and their potentially serious strategic effects is well illustrated by the 2010 hijacking of two Chinese vessels and the brutal murder of their crews in the upper reaches of the Mekong River in the so-called drug Golden Triangle of Southeast Asia. Gangs from disaffected ethnic groups in the region, whose normal modus operandi was largely to extort money from all passing traffic, had evidently decided to seize the vessels and their cargoes, mainly in order to transport a large amount of drugs downriver, in the expectation of much higher rewards. The ferocious reaction of the Chinese population to these murders caused a major diplomatic row between China and Thailand and the suspension of all marine traffic on the river. It resulted in significant Chinese involvement in the policing of the river, and the successful extradition of the perpetrators from Laos (where the crimes were actually committed) constituted a major strategic step forward for the Chinese in their bid to strengthen their position in Southeast Asia.[27]

Assessing the Overall Threat.

When analysts consider the relative importance of different types of nontraditional threats, and indeed of many traditional threats in the shape of interstate wars, the assumption is often that international terrorism represents the gravest challenge to the international system. If, and when, terrorists gain access to weapons of mass destruction, that assumption may turn out to be true. But at the moment, when measured in terms of both financial and human cost, the trade in illicit drugs would currently seem to be much worse and deserving of even more attention and resources.

Moreover, as argued later, there is considerable evidence that terrorist groups are resorting to drug trafficking as a means of raising income and, in some cases, of sapping the strength of their adversaries. Arab penetrations into Central/South America can be seen as revenue raisers for Hamas and Hezbollah, for example. From this perspective, the drug campaign can also be regarded as an indirect defense against terrorism.[28]

Nonetheless, some dismiss the easy analogy of the anti-drug effort as a campaign, or even a war, as a misleading and unhelpful one, not least because it only seems to relate to the supply side of the drug problem and risks fatally neglecting the demand side of the issue to be discussed shortly. The conclusion that often follows is that the illicit trade in drugs should be treated less as a problem to solve and more as a problem to manage; less as a war to win and more as a business model to disrupt.

Those sceptical of the war analogy tend to focus on issues of cost effectiveness that have particular attraction at times of budgetary constraint. They argue, first, for the decriminalization of drug possession and use; and, second, for a strategy of *controlling* the supply of drugs rather than simply seeking to stop it. Some suggest that state authorities themselves may need to assume responsibility for the regulated supply of carefully monitored drugs, much as do Scandinavian countries with the supply of alcohol.

Such critics also argue that calling the struggle against the illicit trade in drugs a "war" may also encourage exaggerated expectations of victory. Certainly in this complex business, it is difficult to establish the metrics by which we can tell who is winning and who is losing because answers depend in large measure on counterfactual assumptions about what would happen if efforts to control the trade were abandoned and partly because the performance indicators are inherently so very complex. The street price of drugs in U.S. and European cities is often used as a performance indicator, since it tends to rise when successful interdiction results in a lowered supply; but there again, so do the profits of the successful DTOs — hardly the objective of the exercise! In fact, there is evidence that drug producers sometimes deliberately withhold supplies themselves as a way of manipulating the street price and so assuring their future income streams.[29]

The U.S. Government target for interdictions is 40 percent. A level of 25 percent was apparently reached in 2009,[30] but most estimates of interception rates in the most contested areas, the Caribbean, the East Pacific, the Atlantic, and the Arabian Sea, are about 20-25 percent for coca-based products and 10-15 percent for opium-based ones.[31] As is so often the case when measuring the effectiveness of governmental action against global crime, statistics are important in driving policy but remain basically insecure.[32] Successful interception rates, for example, are notoriously difficult to measure. They depend on some initial *estimates* of the amount imported each year. The British Serious and Organised Crime Agency (SOCA), for example, estimates that about 25-30 tons of cocaine are smuggled into the UK every year; accordingly, the seizure of 1.2 tons of Venezuelan cocaine in the converted luxury cruiser *Louise* in August 2011 was said to have accounted for 4 percent of the annual total.[33] But the validity of this metric depends on the accuracy of the initial estimate. The problem is aggravated by the fact that many enforcement agencies, especially in West Africa, do not even try to keep reliable statistics of their interception rates.[34]

Moreover, it should be remembered that the seizure of products in transit is only one indicator of success, if the most obvious. More important in many ways might be the effects of the disruption to the DTOs' transportation system and the extra business costs entailed that apparently "failed" operations may cause—but these are much harder to calculate.

But on their own, neither the difficulty of defining success nor the necessity for a hard-headed cost-effective approach to the making and implementation of an anti-drug strategy seem persuasive arguments against thinking of the effort as a long war, for there have been many conventional and unconventional military campaigns where both have been equally true. Wars also often include a very clear economic dimension to them, and so the "war" analogy can easily accommodate the concerted focus on attacking the adversary's business model advocated by many experts in the counternarcotics field.

To conclude, the analogy of the struggle against the trade in illicit drugs as a war does seem, despite its critics, a reasonable one, not least because of its importance, given the scale of threat it represents to the world's peace and prosperity, through, first, the drug trade's association with internal conflict and regional instability;[35] and, second, due to the very high probability that the world's militaries will be significantly involved in it for the foreseeable future.

One of the clear reasons for this is the conclusion of many experts and three-quarters of the American respondents to a recent poll that the United States is losing its war on drugs. This conclusion has resonated across the world. The scale and nature of the drug problem may vary from place to place and from time to time but remains substantial.

While estimates differ widely, the UN Office on Drugs and Crime (UNODC) 2010 Drug Report estimated that there are up to 250 million people accessing illegal narcotics, some 16-38 million of whom are "problem users." The report also estimates there are approximately 21 million users of heroin, morphine, and opium; another 19 million users of cocaine; 52 million consumers of ATS; and between 128 and 190 million cannabis users.[36]

However, many of the trends are moving in the wrong direction. In 2011, opium production in Afghanistan, after a relatively good year in 2010 (thanks largely to providential plant disease), rose by over 60 percent. At the other end of the stability scale, even in tightly regulated and efficiently run Singapore, the Counter Narcotics Bureau had to report that increases in the seizure of heroin, cannabis, methamphetamines, and nimetazepam ranged from 3 percent to a staggering 856 percent. The estimated market value of seizures in the first half of 2010 was S$5.9 million, and increased to S$7.7 million in 2011. There was a 20 percent increase in the number of abusers arrested, which was particularly worrisome in that the biggest increase was in the hard-core methamphetamine abusers, characteristic of the region, but especially in Thailand and the Philippines.[37] In its 2012 report, UNODC predicted a 25 percent rise in illicit drug users by 2050.[38]

The general picture, then, is not an encouraging one; if it is, indeed, a "war," victory is not in sight. Illegal activity on such a scale can hardly fail not to endanger the world's peace and prosperity for producer communities, emerging transit areas, and consumer societies. Clearly, then, given its characteristics and advantages, the military will have to engage seriously in the business of tackling the problem.

THE MILITARY CONTRIBUTION TO THE WAR ON DRUGS

The contribution that the military can make to the war on drugs as part of a wider and comprehensive response varies between the three levels of security threat and between the demand and supply sides of the problem.

The Individual Level: Attacking Demand.

At this level of the problem, the required response is largely a matter of reducing demand. Critics, especially in producer and transit countries, of the hard line on drug production commonly taken in the United States and Europe make the basic point that this trade is actually fueled by demand in their own countries and that this is where the focus of American and European efforts should be. Of the EU's 500 million people, no less than 30 million are drug users. Concentrating instead simply on the supply side in the manufacture, transport, and supply of drugs is held to be the equivalent of bombing Middle Eastern oil wells in order to ease up traffic congestion in London or New York. It is in partial acknowledgment of this point that the Barack Obama administration sought to drop the war on drugs label, and there is justice in this. Instead, there is to be greater emphasis on treatment and prevention; nonetheless, the bulk of the money is still spent on enforcement.[39]

In order to reduce demand, there will be a need to focus on users and abusers, in order fully to understand why some people are uninterested in drugs, others seem capable of keeping their habit under control by keeping it just for recreational use, but a significant minority are capable of neither. Pushing the positive, as well as attacking the negative, would seem to be an important part of such a strategy.

The UNODC concludes that "International drug control efforts cannot be successful in the long term without continuous efforts to reduce illicit drug demand." Accordingly, it is a keen advocate of prevention through persuasion and, where necessary, mass reeducation and rehabilitation through such initiatives as the Global Youth Network. It makes the point that these methods often prove cheaper and more effective in prevention than prosecution and incarceration.[40]

A complementary strand to a strategy of prevention and demand reduction is directed less at reducing demand and more at the profits of meeting it. Here, the focus is on reducing the profits of the supplier. Instead of regarding the campaign against the trade in illicit drugs as a "war," this approach derives from the analogy of attacking it as a business. Decriminalizing drug use, if not drug supply, it is argued, would reduce the glamour of the drug habit and, less probably, demand. More importantly, it would also reduce the profits made by the cartels, and this, in turn, might reduce demand.[41] Thus Portugal's cautious venture into decriminalization of the possession of drugs for personal use, which has apparently reduced problematic drug use, has attracted interest elsewhere in Europe.[42] Indeed, the trend toward partial decriminalization as a significant contribution to winning the war on drugs appears to be gaining momentum elsewhere, too.[43]

The notion that supplying and taking drugs are inherently immoral and should be banned is, in fact, comparatively recent. Drug use, in various forms, was not regarded as illegal until relatively recently, even in Europe. References to the availability of opium were frequent in the advertisements of European newspapers well into the 20th century, and opium-based products were freely available. In Singapore and Malaysia, moreover, the government only banned the sale of opium in 1946.[44] Historically, drug-taking has not been regarded as a criminal act, and there are many who advocate a return to this position.

Jeffery A. Miron, an economist from Harvard, adds the hard-headed point that decriminalization would inject the equivalent of $76.8 billion into the U.S. economy, through savings from the $44.1 billion currently spent on enforcement, plus an estimated $32.7 billion to be derived from a tax regime sufficiently low to discourage unsustainable smuggling.[45]

Treating drugs as simply another commodity that needs to be regulated like cigarettes or alcohol rather than banned raises a number of moral and social issues that are beyond the scope of this Paper. Suffice it to say here that, according to many studies, many of the common drugs are not as harmful, when used recreationally, as either cigarettes or alcohol.[46] Social factors raise other related and legitimate issues. Evo Morales of Bolivia, for example, has argued that coca-chewing is an intrinsic and traditional part of the culture of many in Bolivia, and so justifies growing the crop. Allegedly for this reason, Bolivia has withdrawn from the UN Drug Convention since it does not allow this exception.[47] Peru, the main source of coca leaf, has 61,000 hectares under cultivation, traditionally used in food, tea, and indigenous native ceremonies. Plans to eradicate it, according to Geronimo Villogas, a lawyer for the Association of Coca Growers, are just "a witch hunt against coca growers."[48] Much the same could be said about the cultivation and use of kat in Yemen and elsewhere.

The conclusion that might well be drawn from this is that perhaps selective decriminalization, together with the kind of campaign of dissuasion that has so reduced levels of smoking in Europe, has an important part to play in the campaign against the trade in illicit drugs. Redefining the nature of the product, would, its supporters claim, helpfully shift the campaign from the trade in illicit drugs to the illicit trade in drugs, a potentially quite significant difference. Nor does this appear to be a hopeless quest. The use of illicit drugs across much of the UK, for example, has been steadily falling over the past decade as it falls "out of fashion."[49]

Three things emerge from this: First, nuanced policies of this sort are, indeed, quite hard to reconcile with the analogy of a war on drugs. Second, sensitive and effective regulatory policies are only possible in stable, well-governed societies. Third, decriminalizing the use, if not the supply, of drugs is very unlikely to reduce the need for monitoring and regulation, and for the continued prosecution of the illicit production and supply of harmful drugs. The use of alcohol and cigarettes remains legal in most countries, but for all that, criminal organizations still seek to profit from their illicit supply and so support their continued regulation.[50] Partial decriminalization, in short, is neither generally claimed to be a single answer to the problem, nor to make the attack on the production and transportation of illicit drugs unnecessary.

The mere fact that such opinions exist, whether they are right or wrong, means that attitudes toward the consumption and, indeed, production of drugs vary widely within individual countries and between them. Some authorities have much more relaxed attitudes than others. The result is a singular lack of uniformity of view about the correct response to the problem. Moreover, and with this we begin to move into systemic considerations, nimble DTOs will exploit the differences in regulatory approach taken by countries even within the same region. It is held, for example, that the more relaxed anti-drug policies adopted in parts of Australia have resulted in some DTOs shifting their drug factories there away from the stricter conventions applied in much of Southeast Asia.[51]

Attacking Demand: The Military Contribution.

At first glance, the military would seem to have little role to play in dealing with the drug trade at the critical level of the individual. Indeed, its main focus in this area tends to be on drug prevention within its own ranks. The corrosive effect of drug taking on morale and military effectiveness was vividly highlighted by the experience of the U.S. military services in the late 1960s and 1970s. This illustrates the fact that in democratic societies at least, military organizations tend to reflect the societies they seek to protect, warts and all.

For all that, some have suggested that the military could have a minor role in prevention strategies, through indirectly helping to set social trends by virtue of their own internal control procedures. Whether they can then act as a "school for the nation" in this way depends on their capacity to control the problem within their own ranks. Certainly, given the high regard with which the military is held, at least in most Western societies, failures here are particularly damaging for society as a whole. Moreover, the military may have an important role to play in the strategic communications aspect of the task, as will be discussed later.

The State Level: Attacking Production.

There are two aspects to the requirement to attack the illicit supply of drugs. The first, largely at the level of the state, is the production of the drugs, and the second, at the level of the system, their transportation and delivery to the consumer. The military has a significant role in dealing with both.

Far more countries have the capacity to produce illicit drugs than actually do, and, once again, some analysts make the point that it is as important to understand the reason why some countries that could, do not, as it is to see why those that do, do. This positive/negative approach contributes to a fuller understanding of the broader contextual aspect of the problem.

Different states attach different priorities to crop eradication. Russia, with its large number of addicts and major victims of the trade, traditionally adopts a particularly tough attitude toward eradication in areas of production. In Southeast Asia, crop eradication schemes have likewise proved reasonably successful in reducing heroin production. In other areas, crop eradication has lower orders of priority or is undermined by insufficient means of enforcement.

Apparently successful eradication schemes, however, can have untoward social, political, and economic effects on subsistence producers, often otherwise impoverished peasantry who see opium or coca as no more than an often traditional product, rather more lucrative than others. Crop eradication in Myanmar is claimed to have resulted in a 10-20 percent mortality level and large-scale physical displacement among affected populations. Alienated by the consequences of the destruction of their crops, such growers may well turn against the government that authorized it. These socioeconomic effects can be avoided only if crop eradication is regarded as part of a wider policy of investment in the rural infrastructure, which facilitates the growing of alternative crops like wheat and cotton in Afghanistan. Here, though, crop eradication sometimes appears to have reduced the growing acreage, but at the price of driving the growers into the arms of the Taliban, at least in Kandahar.[52] This approach explains why crop eradication has been more effective in Laos and Thailand than it was in Myanmar, where this approach initially was not taken, though now is.[53] It can, moreover, be prohibitively expensive; opium growing in Afghanistan, for example, provides about 40 percent of the country's gross domestic product (GDP), so filling the gap caused by successful eradication would be expensive indeed.

The socioeconomic problems of crop eradication and the difficulties and expense of enforcement have led some to argue that the cheapest strategy in the bid to attack drug production would be for the government simply to buy the product at prices the DTOs cannot match, which would keep the product out of their hands. The costs of this, it is argued, would be largely, or indeed some would claim wholly, defrayed by subsequent and consequent savings in enforcement. The difficulty here is that many of these savings would be enjoyed by the governments of consumer countries, while the costs of eradication are borne by those of producer countries. Making eradication workable may therefore require the former to subsidize the crop eradication efforts of the latter.

A new problem has appeared that has particularly bad effects on the individual (and therefore on society) and that analytically muddies the difference between the production and transportation sides of the supply dimension of the illicit drug trade. This is the rise in the use and manufacture of methamphetamines (meth), especially in the Asia-Pacific region, where over 70 percent of meth abusers are found and more than half of meth seizures occur. The manufacture of meth depends on the supply of precursor chemicals such as monomethylamine and ethyl phenyl acetate which, in themselves, may be legitimate forms of cargo since they are used in the production of insecticides and cosmetics, respectively, and which are the source of significant and perfectly legal profit to bulk manufacturers, especially in China and India. The conjunction of these two main centers of manufacture means that most of the seizures in illicit precursor chemicals for meth production have taken place in and around East and Southeast Asia.[54]

Law enforcement is, however, another important part of the bid to tackle the production and supply of drugs. Experience shows how necessary it is to arrest and successfully prosecute known producers. But this is often difficult in countries where the police and the judiciary are themselves vulnerable to bribery or physical attack[55] and where the DTOs have the resources to command the services of the best lawyers money can buy. In 1980s Colombia, drugs producers had access to a disproportionately high number of the total of 100,000 domestic lawyers. The result was that they were able to exploit "excessive legality" and operate with judicial impunity.[56] As a first step, regimes need to enact more precise regulatory statutes to deal with such problems and appropriately empower enforcement authorities. Sadly, this is often a painfully slow, heavily bureaucratized and politicized process, especially in the countries that need it most.

A final and equally intractable problem in dealing with illicit drug production is to deal with the financial infrastructure and money launderers who support the trade and often are from outside countries. The drug trade rests on a financial network that operates regionally, if not globally. Dealing with it is not easy for many reasons:

- the intrinsic difficulty in distinguishing between legitimate and illegitimate transactions,
- the varying financial regimes adopted by countries around the world seeking broader commercial reasons to preserve the freedom and confidentiality of banking procedures,
- most of it is transacted on the Web,
- successful prosecutions in this area require collaboration at a transnational level.

Nonetheless, most analysts stress the critical importance of attacking this element of the DTO system.

Attacking Production: The Military Contribution.

The preceding sections shows that attacking drug production may well require crop eradication, regulating the traffic in precursor chemicals, law enforcement, and financial enforcement. The military may need to have a significant role in the first three of these requirements.

Crop Eradication.

Large-scale crop eradication is an area where the military has a major role in the physical destruction of the crops themselves and very often with the initial battles between themselves and the militias and protection teams the DTOs often deploy to guard their drug laboratories, growing areas, and transportation systems. Large-scale efforts are particularly needed in the many areas where drug production is associated with internal insurgencies and conflict, for example in Myanmar, the largest producer of opium after Afghanistan.[57]

Well-funded DTOs have shown they are able to provide themselves with weaponry as good and sometimes better than that of the government forces sent against them. The particularly vicious Zeta gang in Mexico is an especially dangerous opponent, since it reportedly comprises former special forces personnel, both skilled and utterly ruthless.[58] DTOs have been known to deploy "narco-tanks" that are impervious to machine-gun fire and to make copious use of land-mines. Sophisticated assault rifles and other such weaponry are freely available in the United States and shipped south for the DTOs to use against local and ultimately U.S. interests.[59]

Coping with the capacity of the DTOs to defend themselves requires a military or at least a paramilitary response. This has proved a particularly challenging requirement in Colombia, the drugs badlands of northern Mexico, and the *favellas* of Rio de Janeiro, Brazil. Clearing and holding a *favella*, for example, will typically require the deployment of several thousand troops provided with helicopter support, armored personnel carriers, and heavy weaponry, followed by the longer-term deployment of specially trained Pacifying Police Units.[60] Interestingly, the Brazilian Navy, rather than the Army, conducted the November 2011 operation against the Rocinha *favella*, providing commandos, helicopters, and "armor."[61] Such efforts result in a commitment that demands sustained effort and fighting skills beyond the delivery capacity of many weaker states. It is particularly expensive in manpower, most obviously Army manpower, and all the evidence suggests that, without a sustained effort, crop eradication often has limited and temporary effects. Moreover, a cutback in production in a year increases subsequent costs for the consumer and so provides extra incentives to the grower in the following season. Nonetheless, and for all the costs and difficulties, such large-scale military campaigns can be successful, if properly supported and sustained.[62]

Setting up a sustainable agricultural alternative infrastructure to the production of drugs, which clearly needs to be part of the package, becomes difficult, however, when insurgents or terrorists are strong in the growing area and can attack governmental efforts to invest in alternate livelihoods for the growers — as in Afghanistan. For this reason, the military may well be needed for long-term defense of the social and physical infrastructure required for the development of rural economies that do not depend on the growing of drug-related crops.

Tracking Precursor Chemicals.

While the military may provide a useful means of tracking such commodities (or rather the containers in which they are normally carried) as they cross the oceans from initial manufacture to illicit drug laboratories, the task of distinguishing between legal and illegal cargoes is essentially a policing function outside the military's normal sphere of competence.[63] Moreover, the checking of containers is invariably done in port rather than on the high seas.

Law Enforcement.

There are two possible military answers to problems in law enforcement. The first is the imposition of martial law in which the Army[64] assumes responsibility for the arrest and prosecution of drug offenders. This, however, tends further to undermine the legitimacy of civil government, often in countries where it is already weak.[65] Thus Colombia, according to Juan Gabriel Vasquez, one of its most illustrious and articulate sons, is a country characterized by fractious politics in the "long comedy that is Colombian democracy" which made it "a country of impunities . . . that world capital of irresponsibility."[66]

The second approach is security sector reform, a process that usually requires the solicited intervention of outside countries in order to be effective. The Americans and British have both invested in security sector reform in Jamaica as part of their efforts to guard against the domestic effects of drug abuse, but so far with mixed results. In 1986, the U.S. Department of Justice set up the International Criminal Investigative Training Assistance Program (ICITAP) to further this work. Its first assignment was to Colombia, but its work has extended to more than 46 countries, most recently Bantam and East Kalimantan in Indonesia, a country clearly acting as a hub of all forms of maritime crime in Southeast Asia.[67]

What emerges from this is a clear role for the U.S. military, and, in particular, the U.S. Army, in contributing to the professionalization of the local army and paramilitary force which, in fact, have to assume responsibility for the attack on illicit drug production within their own countries. Many armies in Africa and Central and South America have been penetrated and contaminated by the drug cartels and their anti-drug efforts correspondingly undermined. Mexico provides a particularly sad example and, in fact, shows how very necessary is this aspect of security sector reform. The hidden bonus of such capacity building is that the professionalization of local armies will also provide greater security against local social and political instability, assure optimum trading conditions, and provide protection against other forms of international crime, particularly terrorism. It therefore constitutes a significant, if indirect, contribution to security provided by the United States.

The System Level : Attacking the Transportation of Illicit Drugs.

Here attention shifts from production within the state to the transportation of illicit drugs from one state to another, as constituents of the broader international system. Many of the challenges discussed already also apply to the transportation systems that move the product from producer to customer.

Although the production of psychotropic substances may well take place in drug laboratories within the same country as the market, using precursor chemicals that can be purchased over the counter, and in which responsibility for dealing with its transportation is essentially a matter for domestic civil enforcement authorities, the drug trade as a whole relies heavily on the transportation of the precursors and product overland – and to an extent, of course, within particular countries, as well as between them. It is here that the military comes particularly to the forefront.

The transportation of cocaine-based products from Central and South America to their markets in the United States and Europe is intermodal. It goes by land, air, and sea through both the Caribbean Sea, the Eastern Pacific, and Atlantic Oceans. About 20-30 tons of cocaine are transported across the Caribbean every day, for example. An alternate route comes across the Atlantic either going straight for Spain, Ireland, and the UK or, more recently, across on the so-called Highway 10 to West Africa, and either overland or up to the coast of North Africa and across the Mediterranean to southern Europe.

Similarly, in Southeast Asia, illegal trafficking in the precursor chemicals for the manufacture of meth and other ATS is both large scale and primarily moved by sea.[68] Again, opium-based products from Afghanistan and elsewhere usually travel overland through Iran to the Gulf, or to Pakistan, where they are delivered often by small dhows to Yemen, the Horn of Africa, and the United Arab Emirates, from where it is delivered to wider markets in the Gulf and Europe.[69] This transportation system is surprisingly sophisticated, with myriads of transhipments and prearranged pickup points designed to reduce the prospects for successful interception by the authorities.

The sea-borne aspect of this truly global and intermodal transportation system is where navies and coastguards come into their own, but they face many difficulties in taking on this function. Nonetheless, the length of its southern border constitutes a major problem for the United States and provides a major incentive to seek the interception of illicit drugs before they get close, and to do so at sea.

Challenges at Sea.

Navies and coastguards need to be able to detect both the vessels carrying the drugs and the drug cargo within the vessels they search. Neither is easy. First, there is a truly demanding requirement for successful interception. DTOs normally operate with the expectation of profits of about 300 percent. To deal with this, it has been estimated that the rate of interception needs to be about 75 percent. Interception rates, as will be discussed later, are difficult to assess, but they are certainly much lower than this.

Second, the world ocean, as the Russians call it, is a very big place, and the number of assets devoted to the task is relatively small. This applies particularly to the seas around Africa, where only seven countries have the necessary level of GDP (about $10 billion) to operate effective coastguards/navies. The result is a vast area of seven to eight million square kilometers of sea policed by just five frigates, seven medium-range maritime patrol aircraft (MPAs), 18 coastal craft, and 60 limited inshore craft, many of which are barely serviceable. Given the paucity of assets, the marine environment offers peculiar advantages for the smuggler, not least in the capacity to hide. The Caribbean has some 7,000 islands, islets, and cays; the Indonesian archipelago on its own has another 18,000 more. Hence, there is the need for sophisticated maritime surveillance and a judicious mix of numerous inshore patrol craft and longer range ocean going corvettes, frigates, and helicopters. Facing so many other calls on their finite resources, even the U.S. Navy and Coast Guard find a real challenge in dealing with these commitments.

Third, a significant proportion of drugs are not transported by sea at all, they go by air or by land. It is very difficult, even for experts, to arrive at accurate and reliable indications of the relative share of these three modes of transportation, partly because the DTOs vary it all the time in response to the relative successes and failures of interception by the authorities. Nonetheless, so large and so global has the transport of drugs and illegal precursor chemicals become that a large proportion of it must necessarily always go by sea.

Fourth, even when it does go by sea, the small physical size of the product makes detection difficult in many cases. The amount of heroin consumed in a year in the United States, for example, would easily fit into one standard container, and 20 million containers enter the country annually.

Fifth, the DTOs devote considerable ingenuity to the task of concealing the cargoes in ships so that they become extremely difficult to find even when intercepted. Small drug-running dhows operating in the Indian Ocean, for example, often have to be nearly dismantled to locate their heroin or hashish. A particularly nasty device is to conceal illicit cargoes in the primitive, hot, below-deck facilities that serve as their toilets, and which require investigating officers to operate in truly disgusting conditions. Dealing with the ingenious and ever-changing concealment of cargoes requires high levels of training and special resources. It also depends on the extent to which search parties are provided with rules of engagement (ROEs) that allow "destructive search."[70]

Sixth, law enforcement at sea faces a variety of special legal constraints, even though the UN Convention of 1988 on the Illegal Trafficking in Narcotic Drugs and Psychotropic Substances provides a universal legal framework for dealing with the illicit trade in drugs.[71] European navies are limited by the effects of the European Convention on Human Rights, which significantly constrain their capacities and means that suspected drug traffickers cannot simply be handed over for prosecution to other less constrained countries. The level of evidence required for a successful prosecution is the same as it would be for a crime on land, although the conditions for gathering such evidence are often much harder. Such problems are particularly difficult to resolve in sea areas, such as the South and East China Seas, where jurisdiction between coastal countries remains both disputed and strategically sensitive.

Navies operate, moreover, under varying ROEs — the U.S. Navy, for example, is limited by considerations of *posse comitatus*, and so the lead is actually taken by the U.S. Coast Guard, which will also need to place ship-riding legal detachments on Navy warships in order to arrest suspected malefactors. Other navies have to train their generalist personnel simply to do the best job they can. These differences in operation and rules of engagement complicate the prospects for multinational naval cooperation.

Last, law enforcers have to be agile to keep up with the challenges posed by the traffickers. The introduction of self-propelled semisubmersibles (SPSS), for example, is not in itself illegal, although in some cases these may be regarded as "ships without nationality" — and hence open to interception on the high seas. For that reason, the United States has enacted a law making the operation of submersibles a felony and is trying to push this through the Organization of American States (OAS) as well — but so far, only Colombia has followed suit.[72]

How Navies Can Help.[73]

For all the difficulties facing them, navies do make a real contribution to the interception of the maritime transportation of illicit drugs, because of their command and control systems, their platforms, their weaponry and sensors, their capacity for operational planning, and their discipline, training, and general incorruptibility. Some of the better coastguard forces, perhaps a more obvious candidate for the execution of what are, after all, essentially constabulary duties, have such capabilities, too, but usually to a lesser degree. The success of maritime forces rests on the three closely linked and mutually supporting pillars of intelligence, assets, and organization.

Intelligence.

The interception of the passage of drugs at sea is preeminently an intelligence-led operation. There are surprisingly few "cold hits" in which drug shipments are unexpectedly chanced upon.[74] Instead, what is required is "predictive" intelligence in actionable form supplied to those who need it, when they need it. This kind of intelligence usually frames interdiction operations and is absolutely critical to success.

Warships and submarines provide an important covert means of listening in on telephone communications. Sometimes operations that fail to locate drug shipments may, nonetheless, prove a success through intelligence derived from "tickling" the response of the DTOs. Sometimes, too, the enforcement agencies are less interested in securing the cargoes or even the full prosecution of the traffickers than they are in gaining useful intelligence about future operations. Above all, the aim is to gain intelligence about the controllers of these rolling, continuous transportation systems, rather than the poorly paid and often low grade people actually conducting them. In all these ways, long-term strategic intelligence is much more important than short-term tactical intelligence about particular shipments, and it may be well worthwhile to sacrifice the latter in order to gain the former.

Intelligence-gathering is closely associated with the maritime domain awareness that can be generated through the use of MPAs, unmanned aerial vehicles (UAVs), and surface ships.[75] Submarines, perhaps unexpectedly, are particularly valuable, as they provide special advantages in covert intelligence. For example, in 2007, the USS *Annapolis* (SSN760) operating out of Cape Verde provided invaluable intelligence on drugs and people smuggling activities in the area.[76] The number of overall patrol assets, their range, and endurance are critical to success. The resulting data needs to be processed and made available as operational intelligence to those that need it. Navies, with their special and developing experience in the network-central approach, have a great deal to offer, especially when working with others. This is partly a matter of shared technical proficiency, which is ultimately "fixable," and also of protocols and standard operating procedures,[77] matters in which the American tendency to over-classify everything does not help.[78] Policy divergences with coalition partners may be rather more intractable, especially if the United States (or, indeed, any other external power) is suspected of pursuing a unilateralist or national agenda.

The United States has, nonetheless, made important progress in creating the Office of Global Maritime Situational Awareness (GMSA) to encourage interagency information sharing domestically and, to some extent, internationally. The U.S. Department of Transportation has also set up the Maritime Safety and Security Information System (MSSIS) to obtain shipping intelligence, mainly through the Automatic Identification System (AIS). This also sensitizes governments around the world to the existence and scale of the problem. The European Maritime Analysis and Operations Centre-Narcotics (MOAC-N) set up in Lisbon, Portugal, in 2007 is another example of the same kind of thing. It emphasizes the need to share information, seeks to establish links with the authorities in West Africa, and provides a command and coordinating role for interdictions. The electronic tracking and interception in 2007 of the sloop, *Dances with Wolves*, with 1,875 kg of cocaine (worth some 675 million euros) in an operation coordinated by MAOC-N, the UK's Serious Organized Crime Agency (SOCA), Ireland's Joint Drugs Task Force, and the U.S. Drug Enforcement Administration (DEA) are good examples of what can be achieved by this means.

Such coordination is not easy, however. Language, the tendency to over-classify data, differing national standard operating procedures, and institutional rivalries, especially over budgets, all impede the process. Making the need to share information, rather than the need to know it, the default setting in combined anti-drug operations sometimes seems to threaten national protocols and may, in some cases, compromise intelligence sources and so is far from easy. Nor, given the sad fact that some navies, coastguards, and marine police forces are themselves vulnerable to criminal penetration, should information sharing be automatic. Nonetheless, most experts agree that it should be the direction of travel.

Interception Assets.

While at first glance, large numbers of relatively low-tech platforms would seem the obvious means of attacking the DTO's maritime transportation systems, naval capabilities for high-intensity operations can also be very useful in dealing with the technological challenges posed by the drug traffickers. In the Caribbean, the smugglers use commercial vessels and yachts but often resort to so-called go-fast boats that operate at speeds with which few patrol craft or warships can compete. But large long-range helicopters of the sort that can only be carried on large ocean (rather than offshore) patrol vessels, corvettes, and frigates are invaluable for this role. They may need to carry weaponry that can shoot out the engines of boats that will not stop.

Should the smugglers resort to submersibles or even submarines, the more sophisticated radars and surveillance systems are often the most effective means of detecting them. Submersibles are sometimes reconditioned underwater viewing submarines used in coastal tourism or may be constructed out of glass reinforced plastic (GRP) by the traffickers themselves. Something approaching a true submarine has been discovered in Ecuador, with an up and down periscope, an air-conditioning plant, and the like.[79] Submersibles pose a particular challenge, since they are usually best detected by their wake, and stopped ones are much harder to spot. Even with cheap local labor, investing in such transportation technologies is an expensive business for the traffickers and provides a miserable time for the low-grade people who crew them. But the rewards of success can be spectacular, since each such submersible will normally carry at least five tons of cocaine.

It is important to note the deterrent and disruptive effect on the traffickers' business model of interdiction operations. Not infrequently, the mere appearance of a UAV or a helicopter causes the crew of a go-fast boat to jettison their cargo and abandon their mission at considerable cost to the organization — a clear win for the enforcement authorities, even if no cargoes or perpetrators were seized, and no expensive, difficult, and time-consuming trials are possible.[80] In such circumstances, the number and the quality of at-sea assets are key variables in the equation. Hence, the considerable efforts made by the more advanced navies and coastguards to build capacity among smaller states struggling with major gaps between their commitments and the resources with which they have to try to meet them. For this reason, Australia and New Zealand have provided patrol craft for the hard-pressed micro-states of Oceania, and Japan and the United States provided patrol boats to Indonesia in 2007 and 2008.[81]

Organization.

Irrespective of whether the control of the illicit drug trade is seen as a problem to manage or a war to win, the authorities need to develop a clear and effective strategy in order to achieve their ends with the resources available. The military, with its particular expertise in campaign planning, has a great deal of experience to offer in this area. Even the U.S. Coast Guard, the best equipped such force in the world, had apparently lost most of its "contingency planning officers" in the run up to September 11, 2001 (9/11), and its response to that disaster apparently reflected that fact.[82] Most other coastguards are much less well placed. Navies, in short, are often required to act as the main facilitator in developing and helping implement such a strategy.

What has become known as "strategic communications" are clearly an important, though often overlooked, part of such a strategy. Sophisticated navies first have the capacity through their electronic warfare capabilities to take down the communication systems of the DTOs, as the Mexican Navy has recently demonstrated by dismantling the system on which the Zeta cartel relied to coordinate its operations.[83] In general, much of the drug trade relies increasingly on the Internet, so there is a clear and important counternarcotics strand to the battle for the cyber-commons.

All this requires an effective command and control system and efficient data exchange between a variety of civil and military agencies, armies, coastguards, and navies. This, in turn, requires frequently updated and detailed protocols to ensure effective data transfer, which can be secured either by large-scale multilateral agreement or by a complementary series of bilateral arrangements. The latter are particularly necessary, not just in order to authorize rights of hot pursuit and to reconcile judicial legal procedures, but also because of the different operational priorities of individual countries. The United States, for example, is chiefly concerned with the Eastern Pacific routes by which the great majority of the U.S.-bound cocaine is transported. In the Caribbean, the U.S. focus is on the north/south vector of the shipping routes, while its European partners are much more concerned about the east/west vector. The allocation of national maritime enforcement assets naturally reflects these priorities.

Despite these differences, it has proved possible to set up the Caribbean Regional Maritime Agreement (CRMA) of 2001, which, in effect, is an overarching framework for a series of bilateral relationships between the United States and other regional actors, drafted within the auspices of the UN Drugs Convention of 1988. The operational success of such endeavors leans heavily on and hopes to encourage cooperation between maritime enforcement agencies of one sort or another. This facilitates intelligence sharing in the region through the Regional Security System (RSS), the Caribbean Information Sharing Network (CISN), the U.S. Coast Guard's Caribbean Support Tender (CST), and Southern Command's annual Tradewinds exercise.[84] The "West Coast Initiative," launched in 2009, is an attempt to replicate this approach in Africa.[85]

Combined action with other navies and coastguards will also depend on the spread of expertise from the more experienced agencies to the less. Hence, the need for navies/coastguards to participate in capacity-building operations, in the provision of equipment, or in the development of operating skills where standards need to be raised. This may be a delicate business, especially where local states are sensitive about their own sovereignty or where they are seduced by technology and decide they want sophisticated information fusion centers and Command and Control hubs rather than the workaday boarding capabilities they more immediately need. Geography makes capacity building especially important in some cases. Cape Verde, at the end of Highway 10 across the Atlantic, for example, is critical to Europe's interdiction efforts and so attracts a good deal of help.[86]

Facilitative Defense Diplomacy.

As just remarked, soliciting the cooperation of local and neighboring states in the common fight against the drug trade through the establishment of bilateral and multilateral arrangements can be quite tricky politically. Local states may prove sensitive to their sovereignty, and, in some cases, suspicious of the broader purposes of outside states, most particularly the United States. In Central America, the poor relationship between the United States and left wing states such as Venezuela, Bolivia, and Ecuador, makes things difficult. Ecuador's President Rafael Correa, for example, refused to renew a 10-year lease on a U.S. airbase used to conduct surveillance over cocaine-producing areas in the Andes, and the Wikileaks exposure resulted in the expulsion of several U.S. ambassadors who had expressed private concerns about the probity of the police and judicial authorities in these countries.[87]

In some cases, theater engagement, cooperative naval diplomacy, and the offer of training facilities and enforcement capabilities can be important in establishing the framework within which a coordinated campaign can be conducted.[88] The U.S. Navy, for example, has been active in Southeast Asia by encouraging and cooperating with regional navies and coastguards in the establishment of good order at sea regimes. The U.S. Coast Guard has an extensive global engagement program with a particular focus on helping the struggling island states of the Caribbean. The U.S. Coast Guard was a key player in the creation of the CRMA; and in operations in Southeast Asia and the South Pacific.[89]

Once again, capacity-building in counternarcotics has to be seen as part of a much broader picture.

It, and the maritime security scene generally, is an important part of the U.S. Navy's focused engagement in the Gulf, in the Caribbean, around Africa, and in Southeast Asia. But its success depends on political issues much wider than a common concern about the security implications of the illicit trade in drugs.

Putting into effect its ideas of military collaboration in general, and the global maritime partnership in particular, has become a major focus of the current operations of the U.S. Navy. This is intended to serve two complementary post-modern purposes. First, it facilitates the kind of multilateral naval cooperation required to defend the system against the whole range of nontraditional threats such as drug trafficking, terrorism, and piracy. Second, it offers a medium by which the relationship between the naval powers, both with each other and with the United States itself, can be improved.

In this, the U.S. Navy recognizes that the range of requirements also calls for the strongest possible integration of the naval effort with other forces of maritime order, particularly the U.S. Coast Guard. Often, indeed, as both the Japanese and the Americans discovered in the Straits of Malacca, coastguard forces will provide a far more appropriate response to developing situations and thus may well be able to head off the need for more forceful interventions later on. The U.S. Coast Guard is a unique organization unlikely to be replicated anywhere else; nonetheless, it has much to offer in advice on many aspects of maritime security that can be adopted or adapted by anyone else, and it can make that advice available in a manner that represents little threat to the sovereignty of others.[90] By doing so, it indirectly defends the system, while at the same time serving U.S. national interests and contributing to the U.S. maritime outreach.

The U.S. Navy recognizes that the positive encouragement of allied participation in all manner of maritime operations calls for a focused, deliberate, and intelligent maritime assault on all the things that make this difficult at the moment. But against all this, skeptics point to the strategic utility that the United States itself may derive from this kind of focused engagement. Regional allies—once trained up through collaborative exercises, the International Military Education and Training program (IMET), and so forth—may act as force-multipliers, perhaps especially in an era of relative naval decline, by eventually providing additional resources, skill sets, and basing facilities of various kinds. The apparently very collaborative concept of a global maritime partnership may therefore be suspected to serve the more narrow national U.S. interests as well.

This tends to reinforce the argument that coast-guard forces, when they are available, can be more suitable for capacity-building and the establishment of working cooperation than naval forces. They are generally regarded as less sensitive politically and more focused on nontraditional security tasks.[91] But with the exception of the U.S. and Japanese Coast Guards, few of them are as yet capable of substantial capacity-building activities elsewhere, and most concentrate on the policing of their own waters. Moreover, many less developed and smaller countries cannot afford to operate both navies and coastguards, and so the latter's duties are usually carried out by the former.

The focus on interception at sea should not lead to the conclusion that the attack on the delivery of illicit drugs is a matter merely for navies and coastguards. Just as navies (such as the Mexican and the Brazilian) participate in the attack on the production of drugs, so do armies share in the attack on their delivery. The primary reason for this is that DTO transportation systems are intermodal. For this reason alone, armies and air forces are necessarily also heavily, if not as conspicuously, engaged in the mission. To make an obvious, though often over-looked point, the transportation of illicit drugs invariably includes a phase in which they have been moved *within* producer countries.

Moreover, DTO "go-fast" boats and submersibles are usually built on land and operated from land bases and, as such, have been shown to be vulnerable to attack on land. Given the sheer size of the ocean space, it indeed makes much more sense to disrupt drug deliveries at the production end of the supply chain on land rather than to seek to intercept them later by sea. This also reinforces the importance of levels of political agreement about how to deal with the problem between the U.S. Government and the countries where drugs are produced and from which they are exported; as well as the importance of the capacity-building activities of all the U.S. military services, the Army most definitely included.

Perhaps less obviously, the military generally may be the only means of providing a counterpoint in situations where the DTOs get their message across by the systematic intimidation of journalists, the murder of identified bloggers, and the hanging of blood-stained and headless corpses from freeway bridges. Over the past decade, it is estimated that 70-80 journalists have been killed by the cartels in Mexico alone.[92] A successful counternarcotics campaign depends on getting the counternarcotics message across, and the military may well provide a major way of doing this through a coherent effort in strategic communications.[93]

CONCLUSIONS AND IMPLICATIONS FOR THE U.S. MILITARY

Some Tentative Conclusions.

This review suggests the following tentative and generalized conclusions on the relative importance of the military contribution to the counterdrug effort (see Figure 2). The military services seem to have relatively little to offer in the critical campaign to reduce demand, as we have seen. But they do have a good deal to offer to attack both the production and the delivery of illicit drugs. Whether the relative importance of this should be assessed as "medium" or "high" depends very much on particular circumstances, not least the state of alternative means of enforcement when set against the relative size of the challenge presented in the various geographic areas of concern. The success of military-supported eradication campaigns, for example, depends on the extent to which they can be sustained and backed up with infrastructure reform.

	Demand	Supply (Production)	Supply (Transportation)
The Individual	Low		
The State		Medium to High	
The System			Medium to High

Figure 2. Tentative and Generalized Conclusions on the Military Contribution to the Counterdrug Effort.

If they are not, particular eradication campaigns will most likely fail, and the military contribution to them will have been shown to be ineffective. The same kind of consideration needs to inform assessments of the contribution of the military to the campaigns against the delivery of drugs.

The fact that only the most generalized and conditional of verdicts can be arrived at about the importance of the military contribution to the war on drugs simply underlines the essential point that this war is an international and interagency one of many actors, any of which can be crucial in particular circumstances. Even so, it is hard to avoid the conclusion that, in most circumstances, the military is likely to play a key role in the campaign against the production and delivery of illicit drugs.

The fact that it is impossible more exactly to quantify the relative importance of the military contribution to the war on drugs, either when compared to other nonmilitary contributions to the same war or to the relative importance of the other things that the military could be doing with the same resources, is, of course, a major political difficulty for those advocating a greater military focus on the problem. But this difficulty should be alleviated if the real nature of the war on drugs is properly understood.

Some more detailed conclusions also suggest themselves.

A War to be Won?

The consequences of the illicit drug trade for individual, state, and system security briefly reviewed in the first section broadly support the notion that the struggle is sufficiently serious to warrant the phrase "war" and, if for that reason alone, to justify a sub-stantial military role in the response. The importance of the need to address the issue of demand, however, and the extent to which there is need to attack the trade economically, socially, and legally perhaps justifies a wider conception of what "war" means than we have become used to.

The Need for a Holistic Response.

The threat of the illicit trade in drugs needs to be thought of holistically as well as systemically, not least because criminal entrepreneurs show a marked incli-nation to diversify their operations across the spec-trum of economic activity, both legitimate and illegiti-mate.[94] Responding to the multidimensional threats posed by the trade in illicit drugs is a highly complex matter in which there are no simple solutions, no "silver bullets." Instead, it is very much a question of the "twisted rope" of a comprehensive approach that involves all necessary agencies of government and all the necessary governments, too, combined in the full knowledge that none of them on their own can handle the problem, let alone solve it.

All this, it is generally agreed, needs to be inte-grated nationally, regionally, and internationally, and probably in that order. If specific policies operate on separate tracks, inefficiencies, incoherencies, and conflict will occur. It is easy to point out such errors and deficiencies, but it needs to be remembered that the adversary has his organizational deficiencies, too, not least the often ferocious rivalry between different DTOs.[95] Enforcement agencies may have their institu-tional rivalries, but they do not generally resort to the literally cut-throat tactics of Mexican drug cartels.

Horses for Courses.

Similarly, the mix of responses that works in one area may not and probably will not work in another. The issues and problems posed in one region will tend to be surprisingly distinctive from others, even in the business of interdicting the passage of illicit drugs at sea. The island configuration of the Caribbean provides choke points that frame sea-based responses from the U.S. Coast Guard and Navy, which are quite different from the open ocean transits of the Eastern Pacific. In the Caribbean, the 40-knot go-fast boats and submersibles distinguish themselves as drug carriers by their nature and behavior, but in the Arabian Gulf, the problem is to discriminate between hundreds of small and medium dhows, which all look the same and which differ only in their cargo. In the Pacific, in contradistinction to the situation in the Caribbean, the dominance of the meth trade means that the enforcements agencies need to concentrate not on drugs, but on the traffic of precursor chemicals, and order their priorities accordingly.

Part of the Concept of Wider Security.

It is impossible to disentangle the drug problem from its context and the wider issue of conflict and instability.[96] The requirement to provide a potentially exhausting range of responses to the problem becomes more manageable if the drug trade is not isolated from its context but thought of alongside other nontraditional threats to good order, peace, and prosperity as part of the widening concept of security. The difficulty and the expense of examining containers for illicit drugs becomes more manageable, for example, when the need to do so anyway for other smuggled goods, terrorist material, and even illegal immigrants is factored into the equation. Similarly, maritime domain awareness (MDA) for counternarcotics also helps in the struggle against other forms of maritime crime, not the least piracy. British ships deployed to the Caribbean for counternarcotics work have to be there anyway for purposes of hurricane relief and usually perform both roles.[97] In short, actions against the trade in illicit drugs need not and should not be disaggregated from the necessity to deal with other forms of nontraditional threats to peace and prosperity and its costs artificially heightened thereby.

Choosing Time and Target.

There is also an important time dimension in this comprehensive approach. While all these lines of development need to be followed, they do not *necessarily* have to be followed to the same degree and at the same time. The comprehensive approach does not preclude the possibility of identifying particular goals within this broad policy to be prioritized at particular times. Some aspects of the struggle against the trade in illicit drugs can be emphasized at one time, others later. Robert Bonner, for example, argues that the success of the campaign in Colombia in the 1990s was due in large measure to the clarity of the aim, which was purely "to dismantle and destroy the Cali and Medellin cartels — not to prevent drugs from being smuggled into the United States or to end their consumption."[98] In this, the military provided not so much the forces (the Colombian national police were the decisive element), but the campaign planning approach that made sense out of chaos. The removal of the kingpins in the game was critical, since cartels without strong leadership proved vulnerable to collapse.[99] But it is important to note that this did not end the problem; the destruction of the main cartels needed to be exploited with a wide variety of further follow-up activities, on a continuing and probably permanent operational basis.[100]

The Real Long War.

The illicit trade in drugs is a long-term problem of which the world is most unlikely to be free for the foreseeable future but which will need to be controlled over the years, perhaps by a series of carefully targeted campaigns in "a long war." This approach is based on the conclusion that, for all its manifest dangers, the analogy of a war against drugs, or at least the supply of drugs, remains a valid one. If the analogy *is* to be accepted, all concerned need to accustom themselves to the depressing thought that a final victory is most unlikely and that the struggle will be a long and probably unending one, in which the aim might indeed boil down to a campaign to turn a "national security threat" into a "manageable public safety problem," as the latest Presidential Directive on the subject remarks.[101]

Significance for the U.S. Military.

Once the role of the military in general, and of navies in particular, was largely and simply to guard the state, but now, with the impact of globalization, their function has become much wider.[102] Security itself needs to be understood in a much wider way. No new thought, this confirms a trend to which the military services need to accommodate themselves, alongside their preoccupation with regional challengers in the Western Pacific and the Middle East. The resultant choices may be particularly painful at a time of budgetary constraint, but they cannot be avoided.

Although many of the qualities that navies can contribute come as a kind of "free good" through their preparations for more traditional state-centered functions and so may partly defray the cost of setting up or expanding specialist coastguard forces, they nonetheless come at a cost. Counternarcotics operations imply the commitment of resources, especially warships, that, by definition, cannot at the same time be somewhere else doing something else. At a time when many navies, especially in the Western world, are facing severe resource constraints, this is a very serious consideration.

Accordingly, and given the widening range of traditional and nontraditional requirements that navies have to fulfill, choices have to be made and priorities struck between counternarcotics and other roles, and between the main geographic areas on which to concentrate. At a time when most Western navies are facing falling numbers of assets, in terms both of people and platforms and, in consequence, a serious widening of the general gap between resources and commitments, these will not be easy choices to make when it comes to spending and acquisition programs. Perhaps the real and fundamental question that navies face and deal with is that of the extent to which counternarcotics operations are considered a distraction from their real job.

The same point could be extended from warships and other platform assets to the equipment and skill sets needed on board. Counternarcotics operations, for example, require specialist night-vision capabilities, boarding capabilities, training in the search and judicial procedures, and so forth; these, too, come at a cost in lost investment in conventional capabilities.

These considerations apply to the Army, too, only in greater force. The difficulty in imagining a justifying scenario for full-scale high-intensity warfighting on land in the current political and international context would seem to strengthen the U.S. Army's need to rethink its mission priorities, given the demonstrable dangers for U.S. security of continuing to lose the war on drugs and an increasing expectation that an expensive army ought to be able to make a material contribution to success in this war. The fact that the drug trade often flourishes in situations of conflict reinforces the conclusion that military forces generally, and navies in particular, seem increasingly likely to have to integrate nontraditional counternarcotics strategies within their more traditional range of activities, whether they like it or not.[103]

If this is indeed the case, then certain obvious closely related issues arise for the U.S. Army. They include:

- The need to identify the special requirements for the conduct of the war against drugs that are not met through existing warfighting roles and capabilities. Intelligent investment in these special requirements should reduce the prospect of undercutting warfighting capabilities, even at a time of budgetary constraint.
- The Army should make a virtue of necessity by embracing the anti-drug challenge rather than regarding it as an unwelcome distraction from its real job, not least because at a time of strategic uncertainty, there remains a debate about what *is* that real job.

- This monograph has stressed the need for a holistic approach to the drug problem that goes well beyond the making of declaratory statements. The Army's contributions to the war on drugs have to be sufficiently and efficiently coordinated with the other services and governmental agencies.
- The case against the militarization of the war on drugs often implicitly assumes that the United States is fighting this war on its own,[104] but that is far from the case. Accordingly, the U.S. Army needs to be able to interoperate with crucial international partners tactically and operationally. The Army's capacity-building capabilities should be enhanced in order to narrow the gaps with those partners and thus between resources and commitments.
- Bearing in mind such matters as the known deficiencies of the Mexican Army's drug effort and the particular interest of the cartels in recruiting into their ranks ex-military personnel such as the *kabiles* or Special Forces of Guatemala,[105] there is a strong case for more effort to be devoted toward the building of sustainable military capacity in such areas of concern.[106]
- The Army will need to ensure that in the aftermath of the prospective withdrawal from Afghanistan, its institutions and doctrine are fit for the purpose of the counternarcotics campaign. The U.S. Army will need to review its contribution to Joint Doctrine[107] in these new and developing circumstances.
- A final related issue is a conceptual one. The "war on drugs" will be a long one, and the notion that it will conclude in clear-cut victory

seems highly problematic. Instead of expecting decisive victory on one axis of advance, the Army should habituate itself to a slow attritional victory on multiple fronts. For an Army accustomed to aspire to short wars ending in decisive victory, these may be particularly uncomfortable thoughts. The prospect raises the need for some fundamental consideration about military ethos and expectation.

Given the importance of the military contribution to the real long war—the one against the illicit trade in drugs—it is suggested that these questions be seriously considered.

ENDNOTES

1. The U.S. Navy is certainly thinking through the problems and the opportunities. See Ronald O'Rourke, "Navy Irregular Warfare and Counterterrorism Operations: Background Issues for Congress," Congressional Research Service Report 7-5700, Washington, DC: Congressional Research Service (CRS), October 18, 2012.

2. See Joseph Miranda, "The War on Drugs: Military Perspectives and Problems," *DRCNet Special Reports*, available from *www.drcnet.org/military*.

3. Ronald McKie, *Malaysia in Focus*, London, UK: Angus and Robertson, 1963, pp. 55-58.

4. Kenneth N. Waltz, *Man, the State and War*, New York: Columbia University Press, 1959.

5. World Drug Report 2009, New York: United Nations Office on Drugs and Crime (UNODC), 2009, pp. 235-254.

6. "The New Killing Fields: Slaughter and Silence at the Gateway to America," *The Guardian*, September 4, 2010.

7. Steven Dudley, *Walking Ghosts*, New York: Routledge, 2004, is the best analysis of FARC's activities in Colombia. See also "Jamaican Premier Defies US in Battle over Drug Lord," *The Guardian*, May 17, 2010; "Gangster Who Sparked Jamaican Riots Tells US Court: 'I'm Pleading Guilty Because I Am'," *The Guardian*, September 2, 2011.

8. "Tourists Told to Stay Off the Streets as Jamaica's Death Toll Rises," *The Guardian*, May 26, 2010.

9. *Transnational Organized Crime in the West African Region*, New York: United Nations, 2005, p. 3; "Mexican Port Captain Jailed for Alleged Drug Ties," *Associated Press*, May 27, 2010; "Peru President Replaces Senior Policy Officials in Anti-Corruption Purge," *The Guardian*, October 11, 2011.

10. Victoria Bruce and Karin Hayes, with Jorge Enrique Botero, *Hostage Nation: Colombia's Guerilla Army and the Failed War on Drugs*, New York: Alfred A Knopf, 2010; see also Juan Gabriel Vasquez, *The Secret History of Costaguana*, London, UK: Bloomsbury, 2010; and review article by Maya Jaggi, *The Guardian*, June 26, 2010.

11. "California Vote Postpones Rethink on Global Drugs Trade," *IISS Strategic Comment*, London, UK: International Institute for Strategic Studies, November 2010.

12. "Al-Qaida Active in Latin America's 'Triple Frontier'," London, UK: United Press International (UPI), April 4, 2011.

13. "National Security Presidential Directive/SSPD 25," Washington, DC: The White house, February 19, 2003.

14. *Ibid.*, p 3. The claim was repeated in President Obama's Directive of July 2011, where the aim of the counternarcotics campaign was said to be to reduce the drug threat to a "manageable public safety problem." See "New US Effort Targets 'Transnational Organized Crime' as Threat to National Security," *The Washington Post*, July 25, 2011.

15. "Terror and Foreboding as Mexico's Bloody Narcowars Spread South," *The Guardian*, June 29, 2011.

16. Some estimates are rather higher than this. *Globalization 101 News Analysis Case Study: Illicit Drugs and Globalization*, available from *www.globalization101.0rg/news1/drugs_glabalization;* "The Globalization of the Drug Trade," New York: UN Educational, Scientific, and Cultural Organization UNESCO), April 1999, available from *www.unesco.org/most/sourdren.pdf.*

17. Simon Jenkins, "Our 'War on Drugs,' Has Been a Costly Failure. Just Look at Mexico," *The Guardian,* September 10, 2010. The U.S. Drug Enforcement Agency (DEA) puts the figure a little higher at $394 billion. "US SOUTHCOM Shifts as Drug Trade Evolves," *Defense News*, July 29, 2010.

18. "Mexico Claims Victory Over Cartel after Fatal Shooting of Drug Baron," *The Guardian,* July 31, 2010.

19. Dudley.

20. *Achieving the Millennium Development Goals in Africa*, Recommendations of the Millennium Development Goals (MDG) Africa Steering Group, June 2008, New York: UN, 2008.

21. Interviews with Joint Interagency Task Force - West (JIATF-W) staff, October 2011.

22. Robert C. Bonner, "The New Cocaine Cowboys: How to Defeat Mexico's Drug Cartels," *Foreign Affairs,* Vol. 89, No. 4, p. 37.

23. "US and Britain Fear Drugs Are Destabilizing West Africa," *The Guardian,* December 15, 2010. The release of the *Wikileaks* cables has shown the damagingly low opinion held by these two countries of the enforcements agencies in countries such as Ghana and Sierra Leone.

24. "US Trains Africans to Fight Al-Qaida," London, UK: UPI Staff Writers, May 18, 2010.

25. "West Africa's 'Cocaine Coast'," *IISS Strategic Comments,* Vol. 17, May 2011.

26. "Drug Barons Accused of Destroying Guatemala's Rainforest," *The Guardian,* June 13, 2011.

27. "Drug Traffickers Kill 13 Chinese Crewmembers after Hijacking on Mekong River," *The Maritime Executive,* October 10, 2011; "China Sentences Four to Death for Mekong Murders," *The Straits Times,* November 7, 2012.

28. Testimony of Michael Braun, DEA Chief of Operations to House International Relations Committee, Washington, DC: House of Representatives, March 30, 2006.

29. "Insurgents Stockpiling Opium to Fix Global Heroin Prices, UN Drug Chief Told NATO," *The Guardian,* December 21, 2010.

30. U.S. Coast Guard (USCG) Interviews, Washington, DC, September 2010.

31. In the United States, the counternarcotics metrics are synthesized in the Consolidated Counter Drugs Data Base to which all the agencies report. But their metrics change; some include estimates of dumped cargoes, while others do not. Partner nations in the Caribbean do not necessarily use the same metrics.

32. Peter Andreas and Kelly M. Greenhill, eds., *Sex, Drugs and Body Counts: The Politics of Numbers in Global Crime and Conflict,* Ithaca, NY: Cornell University Press, 2010.

33. "Drugs Bust on Boat Nets 1.2 Tonnes of Cocaine," *The Guardian,* August 4, 2011.

34. *Transnational Organized Crime in the West African Region,* p. 12.

35. Robert J. Caldwell, "A War We Cannot Afford to Lose," *San Diego Union-Tribune,* May 25, 2008.

36. UNODC, *2010 World Drug Report,* New York: UN, p. 132.

37. BBC News, "Afghan Opium Production 'Rises by 61%' Compared with 2010," CNB Drug Situation report available from *www.bbc.co.uk/news/world-south-asia-15254788;* "Biggest Haul of Ice Seized in Two Day Crackdown," *The StraitsTimes,* November 15, 2011.

38. "Number of Illicit Drug Users to Increase by 25%, UN Predicts," *The Guardian,* June 27, 2012.

39. USCG Interviews, Washington, DC, September 2010.

40. *International Narcotics Control Board Report 2009,* New York: UN, February 2010, pp. iii, 1-13.

41. Drug legalization is increasingly seen as part of the solution, but remains controversial. See *The Guardian,* August 5, 2008. Thus, Juan Gabriel Vasquez, who argues that a puritanical America will never legalize drug use, thereby condemning the producer nations to be "drowned" in internal wars forever. *Ibid.* The UN's Drug Czar, Antonio Maria Costa, Executive Director of UNODC, is vehemently against legalization. See Jenkins. The idea of selective decriminalization, especially of marijuana, is often discussed, but the failure of "Proposition 19," in California in November 2010, suggests that substantive moves in this direction will be a long time coming. See *IISS Strategic Comments,* November 2010. Moreover, the dangers of piecemeal country-by-country decriminalization are obvious and another example of the way in which effective responses can only be regional, or better still, global.

42. "Lib Dems Want Inquiry into Decriminalizing Drug Possession," *The Guardian,* August 5, 2011; Peter Wilby, "Many Agree, None Act: To Ease Untold Misery, Legalise Drugs,"*The Guardian,* June 2, 2011.

43. "Violence Fuels Debate on Drugs Legalisation," *IISS Strategic Comments,* Vol. 18, Comment 12, March 2012; Alan Travis, "Decriminalise Drug Use, Say Experts after Six-Year Study," *The Guardian,* October 14, 2012.

44. Ronald McKie, *Malaysia in Focus,* London, UK: Angus and Robertson, 1963, p. 56.

45. See, for example, his Jeffrey A. Miron, "The Budgetary Implications of Marijuana Prohibition in the United States," June 2005, available from *www.prohibitioncosts.org/mironreport/*.

46. "Alcohol 'More Lethal' Than Heroin, Cocaine," *The Straits Times*, November 2, 2010.

47. "Bolivia to Withdraw from UN Drug Convention," *Latin American Herald Tribune*, July 3, 2011.

48. *Canada*, Reuters, November 26, 2010.

49. "Downwards Trend in Substance Use as Drugs Fall Out of Fashion," *The Guardian*, September 28, 2012.

50. *Transnational Organized Crime in the West African Region*, p. 28.

51. "Drug Gangs Exploit 'Soft' Australian Laws," *The Straits Times*, December 2, 2010.

52. Anand Gopal, "The Battle for Afghanistan: Militancy and Conflict in Kandahar," Washington, DC: The New America Foundation, 2010, p. 5.

53. Andrew R. C. Marshall, "Myanmar Declares War on Opium," *Reuters Special Report*, February 17, 2012.

54. Interviews with JIATF-W, September 2011; UNODC, Annual Report Questionnaire Date/Delta; WCO Customs and Drugs Report 2006, June 2007. Afghan heroin has its precursors too, mainly acetic anhydride (AA), which comes in mainly from Japan, South Korea, and China.

55. "'I Was Told I'd Be Killed' — The Anti-Drug Judge under 24-Hour Protection," *The Guardian*, January 5, 2011.

56. "Born in Bogota and . . . a lawyer by profession, that oh so frequent combination in my centralist and pettifogging country," in Juan Gabriel Vasquez, *The Secret History of Coastaguana*, London, UK: Bloomsbury, 2011, p. 99; Dudley. The problem of excessive legality, moreover, is widespread. The Jamaican government, for example, has resisted American requests for extradi-

tion on the grounds that the evidence has been obtained through illegal telephone tapping."Jamaica's Beleaguered Leader to step Down," *New York Times,* September 25, 2011.

57. "Big Surge in Drug Production," *The Straits Times,* June 24, 2010.

58. "Terror and Foreboding as Mexico's Bloody Narcowars Spread South," *The Guardian,* June 29, 2011; "Mexico Drug Crisis a Boon for Defense Deal," London, UK: UPI, June 6, 2011.

59. "Smuggled Weapons; Bigger the Better," *Houston Chronicle,* May 29, 2011; BBC News, "Mexican Army Destroys Drug Cartel 'Narco Tanks'," June 6, 2011; "Three Soldiers Die in FARC Minefield in Northwestern Colombia," *Latin American Herald Tribune,* September 27, 2011.

60. "Troops to Occupy Brazilian Slum through October," CNN, November 30, 2010.

61. "Brazil Expels Drug Gangs in Rio's Biggest Slum," *The Straits Times,* November 14, 2011.

62. "Success of Rio's Favella 'Pacification' Shows in Boredom of A&E Room," *The Guardian,* April 2, 2011.

63. Interview with JIATF-W Staff, October 2011.

64. Although such operations are usually Army led, this is not always so. "Report: Mexican Drug Lord Killed in Shootout," *CNN News,* May 27, 2010. In this instance, the Navy was used for such purposes, because it was, according to Bonner, p. 40, "the country's least corrupt government institution."

65. "Jamaican Army Accused of Murdering Civilians," *The Guardian,* May 28, 2010. The need for this to be the function of a properly trained police force is strongly argued in Robert C. Bonner, "The New Cocaine Cowboys: How to Defeat Mexico's Drug Cartels," *Foreign Affairs,* Vol. 89, No. 4. Nonetheless, Bonner makes the point that the Mexican military was "one of the country's few reliable institutions," p. 40. Moreover, the violence associated with such campaigns will often antagonize liberal activists

within the country. Luiz Hernandez Navarro, "A War on Drugs? No, It Is a War on the Mexican People," *The Guardian*, August 13, 2010.

66. Juan Gabriel Vasquez, *The Secret History of Coastaguana*, London, UK: Bloomsbury, 2011, pp. 155, 157.

67. Alban Sciascia, "East Kalimentan: A New Front for Regional Maritime Security?" *RSIS Commentary*, Vol. 30, 2011.

68. UNODC, Annual Report Questionnaire Date/Delta; WCO Customs and Drugs Report 2006, June 2007.

69. "The RN: A Global Force," available from *www.newsdeskmedia.com/files/RNGF%202010-11%20LoRes.pdf*; interviews with Commander Keith Wynstanley, Royal Navy (RN), and other RN staff officers, July/August 2010.

70. Search parties without such rights have to repair any damage or disruption their searches may have caused. This can be extraordinarily time and resource consuming. Interview of Commander K. Wynstanley, RN, August 2010.

71. UNODC, *UN Crime and Drug Conventions: Drug Control Treaties and Related Resolutions 2007*, New York: UN, 2007.

72. USCG Interviews, Washington, DC, September 2010.

73. Perhaps the first requirement is not to traffic drugs themselves. Even the best navies may be open to this form of abuse. "Former Asylum Seeker Used Navy Ship to Smuggle Cocaine," *DailyTelegraph*, June 19, 2010. The occasional naval problem, though, seems dwarfed by the contamination in some armies and air forces. "Dominican Official Arrested," *Miami Herald*, December 3, 2010; "Drug Bust Shows Argentina-Europe Trafficking Ties," *New York Times*, January 29, 2011; "Cambodia Arrests Generals for Drug Trafficking," *Vietnam News*, November 2, 2011.

74. Interviews as USCG Headquarters, Washington, DC, September 2010.

75. "Brazil Unmanned Aircraft Hunt Drug Gangs," London, UK: UPI, July 13, 2011.

76. "A US Sub in Cape Verde against Narco-trafficking," *Afrique En Ligne*, Praia, Cape Verde, November 16, 2007; for another example, in the Caribbean, see "Submarines Join Fight against Caribbean Drugs," *Amigoe*, Netherlands Antillies, Willemsted, March 17, 2008.

77. See Paul T. Mitchell, *Network Centric Warfare: Coalition Operations in the Age of US Military Primacy*, Adelphi Paper No. 385, London, UK: IISS, 2006.

78. This was even a problem in the tsunami relief operation. See Bruce Elleman, *Waves of Hope: The US Navy's Response to the Tsunami in Northern Indonesia*, Newport RI: Naval War College Press, 2007, p. 72.

79. DEA release March 7, 2010. The expertise came from Asia. This submarine could carry up to 10 tons of cargo and probably cost less than a million dollars to build. "DEA: Seized Submarine a Quantum Leap for Narcos," *Seatlle PI*, Associated Press, July 4, 2010.

80. The Dutch warship *HMNLS Van Speik* reported one such incident. Among the drug cargo dumped was $500,000 in dollar bills. A "go-fast" boat will normally carry 1-1.5 tons of cocaine. Confidential interviews, 2010.

81. Civil Maritime Analysis Department, *Worldwide Threat to Shipping*, Washington, DC: Office of Naval Intelligence, December 26, 2007, January 23, 2008.

82. Letter by Captain Bruce Stubbs, U.S. Coast Guard, to the *Washington Post*, December 1, 2001.

83. "Mexican Navy Dismantles Zeta Communication System," *Miami Herald*, September 8, 2011.

84. Testimony of General James T. Hill, Special Operations Command, before the House Armed services Committee, 108th Cong., 2nd Sess., March 24, 2004.

85. UN Press Release, July 8, 2009.

86. Interview, RN Naval Staff, October 2010.

87. "US Expels Envoy from Ecuador, President Correa Slams US," Bloomberg, April 7, 2011.

88. "Cuba and UK in Anti-Drug Smuggling Talks," *BBC News*, November 15, 2010. In this case, the Type 42 destroyer *HMS Manchester* provided a useful facilitative role. "Algeria and US Conduct Joint Maritime Exercises," *Jane's Defence Weekly*," October 14, 2009.

89. Angela Henderson, "US Coast Guard Hosts Oceania Military Leaders for Maritime Security Talks," *Coast Guard News*, March 23, 2009.

90. The Model Maritime Service Code issued by the U.S. Coast Guard in 1995, now being reworked, is a good example of this since it is intended to "assist other nations in developing a Maritime Force to help them meet the changing needs of the 21st century."

91. For instance, the time on task of U.S. Coast Guard vessels in the Caribbean is typically twice as long as U.S. Navy warships rotated there from other duties for the purpose. USCG Intelligence.

92. Alma Guillermoprieto, "Mexico: Risking Life for Truth," *New York Review of Books*, November 22, 2012.

93. "Mexico's Drug Cartels Have New Target: Social Media," *Toronto Star*, September 16, 2011.

94. *Transnational Organized Crime in the West African Region*, pp. 17-18.

95. One of the most worrisome aspects of the situation in northern Mexico was the extent to which the local DTOs seemed at times to be able to suspend their own differences in common cause against the government. The sheer size of the market for illegal drugs in the Asia-Pacific region and its dominance to date

by the ethnic Chinese reduces such conflict and rivalry here, too, but the intrusion of other DTOs and more market pressure may change this. Interviews at JIATF-W, October 2011.

96. *Transnational Organized Crime in the West African Region*, pp. 2-4; Paul Rexton Kan, *Drugs and Contemporary Warfare*, Washington, DC: Potomac Books, 2009.

97. It is worth noting that the offshore patrol vessels (OPVs) often advocated for counternarcotics work could not safely deal with the sea states associated with hurricanes, while also carrying the larger crews and sometimes helicopters needed for effective counter-drug interdiction.

98. Bonner, p. 42.

99. *Ibid.*, p. 44.

100. Colombia, for example, is thought to have produced 650 tons of cocaine in 2002. The internal situation has much improved since then, but it still produced 410 tons in 2009. "A Country Transformed, But Still a Dark Side to Uribe's Colombia," *The Guardian*, August 7, 2010; "Violence Returns to Colombia," *Newsweek*, September 20, 2010.

101. "New US Effort Targets 'Transnational Organized Crime' as Threat to National Security," *The Washington Post*, July 25, 2011.

102. The widening of the concept of security is dealt with in Barry Buzan, *People, States and Fear*, 2nd Ed., New York: Harvester Wheatsheaf, 1991; and Jessica Tuchman Mathews, "Redefining Security," *Foreign Affairs*, Spring 1989.

103. This argument is cogently made in Kan.

104. See, for example, Miranda, *The War on Drugs*.

105. Robert Culp, "Strategy for Military Counter Drug Operations," *Small Wars Journal*, January 24, 2011; "Army's Role in Mexico Drug War Questioned as Generals Held," *Agence France Presse*, May 21, 2012; "Central America Confronts the Drug Gangs," London, UK: IISS, *Commentary* Vol 18, Commentary 23, August 2012.

106. Here it might well be worth investigating why some navies have a consistently better anti-drug record than some armies. "Mexican Navy Shoots Dead Brutal Drug Cartel Leader—But Body Goes Missing," *The Guardian,* October 10, 2012.

107. *Joint Publications 3.07.4, Joint Counterdrug Operations,* Washington, DC: Joint Chiefs of Staff, June 13, 2007.

www.ingramcontent.com/pod-product-compliance
Lightning Source LLC
Chambersburg PA
CBHW070613290526
45790CB00002B/890